For God alone I wait silently;

my deliverance comes from him.

He only is my rock of deliverance,

my strong tower, so that I stand unshaken.

From Psalm 62

Do not be anxious about food and drink to keep you alive and about clothes to cover your body. Surely life is more than food, the body more than clothes . . . Do not be anxious about tomorrow; tomorrow will look after itself. Each day has troubles enough of its own.

Jesus' words in Matthew 6

The Lord is faithful to his promises,
and everything he does is good.
He helps those who are in trouble;
he lifts those who have fallen.

From Psalm 145

The Lord's arm is not too short to save
nor his ear too dull to hear.

From Isaiah 59

'For I know the plans I have for you,'
declares the Lord, 'plans to prosper you and
not to harm you, plans to give you hope and
a future. Then you will call upon me and
come and pray to me, and I will listen to
you. You will seek me and find me when you
seek me with all your heart.'

From Jeremiah 29

I *will never leave you or desert you.*

From Hebrews 13

Are not two sparrows sold for a penny?
Yet without your Father's knowledge not one of
them can fall to the ground. As for you, even the
hairs of your head have all been counted. So do
not be afraid; you are worth more than any
number of sparrows.

Jesus' words in Matthew 10

Wait quietly for the Lord, be patient till
  he comes;
do not envy those who gain their ends,
or be vexed at their success.

From Psalm 37

If I said that my foot was slipping,
your love, Lord, continued to hold me up.
When anxious thoughts filled my heart,
your comfort brought me joy.

From Psalm 94

Cast all your anxiety on him because he
cares for you.

From I Peter 5

Do not be fearful or discouraged, for
wherever you go the Lord your God
is with you.

From Joshua I

Do not be anxious, but in everything make your requests known to God in prayer and petition with thanksgiving. Then the peace of God, which is beyond all understanding, will guard your hearts and your thoughts in Christ Jesus.

From Philippians 4

Do not be afraid—I will save you.

I have called you by name—you are mine.

When you pass through deep waters,

I will be with you;

your troubles will not overwhelm you.

When you pass through fire, you will not be
burnt;

the hard trials that come will not hurt you.

From Isaiah 43

T*he Lord himself will be with you; he will*
not let you down or forsake you. Do not be
afraid or discouraged.

From Deuteronomy 31

What, then, can separate us from the love of Christ? Can trouble do it, or hardship or persecution or hunger or poverty or danger or death? . . .

For I am certain that nothing can separate us from his love: neither death nor life, neither angels nor other heavenly rulers or powers, neither the present nor the future, neither the world above nor the world below—there is nothing in all creation that will ever be able to separate us from the love of God which is ours through Christ Jesus our Lord.

From Romans 8

Peace I leave with you; my peace I give you. I do not give to you as the world gives. Do not let your hearts be troubled and do not be afraid.

Jesus' words in John 14

God gives strength to the weary...

those who hope in the Lord

will renew their strength.

They will soar on wings like eagles;

they will run and not grow weary;

they will walk and not be faint.

From Isaiah 40

Published by
Lion Publishing plc
Sandy Lane West, Oxford, England
ISBN 0 7459 2964 8
Lion Publishing
850 North Grove Avenue, Elgin, Illinois 60120, USA
ISBN 0 7459 2964 8
Albatross Books Pty Ltd
PO Box 320, Sutherland, NSW 2232, Australia
ISBN 0 7324 0826 1

First edition 1994

Picture acknowledgments
Lion Publishing: waterfall, gate, yacht; Oxford Scientific
Films: bald eagle; Willie Rauch: all others.

Scripture acknowledgments
Scripture quotations are taken from the *Good News Bible* ©
American Bible Society, New York, 1966, 1971 and 4th
edition 1976, and published by Bible Societies/
HarperCollins; *The Holy Bible, New International Version*:
copyright © New York International Bible Society, 1973,
1978, 1984, and published by Hodder & Stoughton Ltd; and
the *Revised English Bible* © 1970/1989 by permission of
Oxford and Cambridge University Presses.

Bible verses selected by Joyce Currer

A catalogue record for this book is available
from the British Library

Library of Congress CIP Data applied for

Printed and bound in Hong Kong